Posters

Posters

Attilio Rossi

Paul Hamlyn

LONDON · NEW YORK · SYDNEY · TORONTO

Translated by Raymond Rudorff from the Italian original

I manifesti

© *1966 Fratelli Fabbri Editori, Milan*

This edition © copyright 1969
THE HAMLYN PUBLISHING GROUP LIMITED
LONDON · NEW YORK · SYDNEY · TORONTO
Hamlyn House, Feltham, Middlesex, England

S.B.N. 600012611

Text filmset in Great Britain by
Yendall & Co. Ltd, London

Printed in Italy by
Fratelli Fabbri Editori, Milan

Contents

FROM PRINTED NOTICE TO POSTER

The immediate ancestor of the modern poster was the printed notice, an announcement or advertisement which was almost exclusively typographical in composition, though it might be embellished with vignettes and various heraldic devices. Such printed notices were produced and displayed on walls and hoardings both before and after the invention of lithography, which gave rise to the modern poster.

From the technical point of view, lithography produced excellent results from the beginning, thanks to the simplicity of the process, which often encouraged artists to draw directly on to the stone, and to a close and happy collaboration between the printer and artist. When lithography was invented (by Senefelder, in 1793) the intention was to reproduce works of art more cheaply than by the traditional methods of wood and metal engraving; but it was to attract the attention of such artists in their own right as Daumier, Manet, Gavarni and Toulouse-Lautrec. The result was that many early posters were of considerable—

and original—artistic merit. But for a better understanding of the success of lithography and the felicitous collaboration between lithographers and artists, it is necessary to begin earlier in the 19th century.

This was a period in which the technical and industrial results of previous discoveries became apparent. At the same time, political conditions, especially the frequent upheavals in France, gave rise to a proliferation of posters, notices and proclamations which stimulated the art of political caricature in lithographs by Daumier, Gavarni, Doré and many others.

In 1833 Brisset invented the rotary lithographic press, which is still used for art lithography today; this made it possible for large prints to be made from stone and, soon afterwards, zinc plates. Three years after Brisset's invention, Engelmann perfected the chromolithographic process. The inventions of Senefelder and Brisset, complemented by chromolithography, enabled Chéret and his printer, Chaix, to produce an enormous number of posters which are still admired today. Other important events in the history of printing were the invention of the flat lithographic machine and the use of grained zinc plates; after this, several posters could be printed at a time, some as much as ten yards long.

This book does not pretend to be a comprehensive history of poster art: it is obviously impossible within such a limited space to trace the ancestry of the modern poster in any great detail. But it is worth briefly recounting the slow evolution of the poster as a means of information or cultural communication, or a means of propaganda and commercial publicity. The most ancient precursors of the poster are exciting evidence of man's astuteness and intelligence in his dealings with others, whether in love, commerce or politics.

Egyptian and Sumerian hieroglyphic tablets are the earliest known ancestors of the Western poster. For our own purposes the Chinese can be ignored. The ancient Romans not only inherited these means of communication but developed them, using other materials such as bronze and copper, and provided poster-space: uniform whitewashed rectangles set on walls at cross-roads and in public squares. Pompeii is full of such notices, which often display a considerable command of advertising language. Some are menacing in tone, mentioning evil omens, and were put up by angry private citizens tired of seeing unsolicited and unwelcome writings appear on their walls outside the prescribed spaces. One such warning referred to an election candidate for, after the usual 'please do not write here', it threatens 'disgrace to the

1.   Jules Chéret. *La Diaphane, Poudre de Riz, Sarah Bernhardt*. 1890. Civica Raccolta stampe Bertarelli, Milan.

2. Jules Chéret. *Théâtrophone*. 1890. Bibliothèque des Arts Décoratifs, Paris.

1. Jules Chéret. *La Diaphane, Poudre de Riz, Sarah Bernhardt.* 1890. Civica Raccolta stampe Bertarelli, Milan. © by SPADEM; Paris, 1967. A typical advertising poster of a kind that might well be found today; the coquettish gesture of the young woman of the 'nineties is not very different from that of a modern woman.

2. Jules Chéret. *Théâtrophone*. 1890. Bibliothèque des Arts Décoratifs, Paris. © by SPADEM; Paris, 1967. A carefully controlled composition, less casual than the previous example. Chéret's favourite model, the beautiful Charlotte Wiche, is in the foreground.

3. Jules Chéret. *La Loïe Fuller, Folies-Bergère*. 1893. Bibliothèque des Arts Décoratifs, Paris. © by SPADEM; Paris, 1967. The quintessence of Chéret's type of design, with the 'woman-flower', the dancer Loïe Fuller, amid the whirlwind of flowing draperies for which she was famous.

4. Henri de Toulouse-Lautrec. *Divan Japonais.* 1892. Civica Raccolta stampe Bertarelli, Milan. The necessities of the composition led Lautrec to represent the star, Yvette Guilbert, without her head. All that was needed to suggest her personality were her famous long gloved arms. The two spectators in the foreground are Jane Avril and the critic Edouard Desjardins.

5. Henri de Toulouse-Lautrec. *Jane Avril, au Jardin de Paris.* 1893. Musée Toulouse-Lautrec, Albi. Despite the tragic face of the main figure, this poster is one of Toulouse-Lautrec's most successful compositions. The large foreground of orchestral motifs has been harmoniously blended into the curve of the musical instrument.

3. Jules Chéret. *La Loïe Fuller, Folies—Bergère*. 1893.
Bibliothèque des Arts Décoratifs, Paris.

4.   Henri de Toulouse-Lautrec. *Divan Japonais*. 1892.
Civica Raccolta stampe Bertarelli, Milan.

5. Henri de Toulouse-Lautrec. *Jane Avril, au Jardin de Paris.* 1893. Musée Toulouse-Lautrec, Albi.

candidate whose name shall be written on this wall. May he never succeed.'

The long evolution of this means of communication can be traced, thanks to such evidence as a column, found at Herculaneum in 1897, which was still covered with notices written on papyrus, one pasted over the other; an Italian poster of 1630 illustrated by a vignette and announcing that one Gian Giacomo Mora had been condemned to death; and the edict which informed the Paris populace that the execution of Louis XVI was to take place at noon on Monday 21 January, 1793, in the Place de la Révolution.

The first real posters were the monopoly of Church and State; the Church used them to announce the granting of indulgences, the State to recruit volunteers. The first paper battle between conflicting notices occured during the French Revolution.

A ruling providing for a corporation of 40 billstickers, who were required to be able to read and write, and the Le Chapelier law of 1791, which allowed private individuals to put up notices as long as they used coloured paper (black type on white paper being exclusively reserved for the authorities) were evidence that even in the 18th century the professions of public crier, towncrier and herald were being seriously menaced by the competition of wall-posters.

Two laws served as a basis for similar legislation in other countries: the law of 1818 which decreed that all posters stuck on the walls of Paris must have a stamp affixed to them; and the law of 1881 (also French) which regulated the placing of posters.

Careful study of old posters (some are highly amusing) makes it possible to trace the slow formation of a synthetic, informative style and the gradual evolution of the psychologically persuasive language of publicity. It also reveals the progressive diminution of textual content and the growth of the original vignette into a highly-coloured design that dominated the entire composition. At which point the notice has been entirely transformed—into the modern poster. Such a study might include the legal aspects of poster advertising, beginning with the first laws regulating bill-sticking; and, on the technical plane, the invention of lithography and chromolithography and the first experiments in colour photography. Given the rarity of many examples, it is difficult to trace the evolution of poster art with exactitude; hence the otherwise inexplicable omissions in the beautiful exhibition '*Cinq Siècles d'Affiches Illustrées Françaises*' of 1953.

The modern poster's points of departure are well known: Rouchon's famous posters and colour prints, which began to be circulated in about 1850; and the 'booksellers' posters' of 1830-1870—enlarged book illustrations placed in windows to publicise new books.

The exhibition '*Le Début de l'Affiche Moderne*', covering the period from 1889 to the present day, showed works by all the artists who evolved the modern poster, though many were only sparsely represented: Jules Chéret's *Saxoléine*, Pierre Bonnard's *France-Champagne*, Toulouse-Lautrec's *Jane Avril, Candieux* and *Aristide Bruant*, Firmin Bonisset's *Chocolat Meunier;* also works by Eugène Grasset, Mucha and a few others, including Cappiello's beautiful *Corset le Furet* of 1904 and his less successful *Moutarde Savora* of 1930. Although they were represented in later exhibitions, some indispensable names were missing: Forain, Steinlen, Sem, O'Galop (the creator of the Michelin *Bibendum*), and many others. The period 1914-1939 was even more poorly illustrated, for Cassandre's work was represented by only one poster and there was nothing by Sepo.

In the exhibition '*Cent Ans d'Affiches: La Belle Epoque*' (1964), organised for the centenary of the Union Central des Arts Décoratifs in the Pavillon Marsan of the Louvre, stress was laid upon the documentary rather than the plastic aspects of poster design; the result was that nothing new was learned

6.   Pierre Bonnard. *France Champagne*. 1892.
Bibliothèque des Arts Décoratifs, Paris.

6.   Pierre Bonnard. *France-Champagne*. 1892. Bibliothèque des Arts Décoratifs, Paris. © by ADAGP; Paris, 1967. Effervescence, communicated by a compositional arabesque, and the frizzy champagne-coloured hair of the girl stress the two main qualities of the product advertised. Although this was his first poster, Bonnard succeeded in devising extremely clever visual metaphors.

7.   Henri de Toulouse-Lautrec. *La Revue Blanche*. 1895. Civica Raccolta stampe Bertarelli, Milan. Missia, the wife of Thadée Natanson, the director of the *Revue Blanche,* was Lautrec's model for this poster. The figure is represented diagonally, in the act of making a sudden gesture, as though caught in a snapshot.

8.   Henri-Gabriel Ibels. *L'Escarmouche*. 1893. Civica Raccolta stampe Bertarelli, Milan. The poster was made for a well-known weekly which carried illustrations by many famous artists of the day. Its lack of boldness and use of chiaroscuro are not the result of incompetence: a note at the bottom makes it clear that the poster was not meant to be displayed out of doors.

9.   Auzolle. *Cinématographie Lumière*. 1896. Bibliothèque des Arts Décoratifs, Paris. The early days of the cinema—the fascination of moving pictures, the thrill of a darkened auditorium—are brilliantly evoked by this poster.

7.   Henri de Toulouse-Lautrec. *La Revue Blanche*. 1895.
Civica Raccolta stampe Bertarelli, Milan.

8.   Henri-Gabriel Ibels. *L'Escarmouche*. 1893. Civica Raccolta stampe Bertarelli, Milan.

9.   Auzolle. *Cinématographie Lumière*. 1896. Bibliothèque
des Arts Décoratifs, Paris.

about the history of the poster. In Italy, the '*Mostra del Manifesto Italiano nel Centenario del Manifesto Litografico*' overcame all difficulties and, after a careful process of identification and cataloguing, produced a reliable catalogue of the posters exhibited.

In the second half of the 19th century, the poster assumed its definitive format, still valid today, thanks to the contribution of two great artists: Bonnard and Toulouse-Lautrec. Although they were unalike in temperament, their poetic talent and ability to create synthetic designs made them the outstanding successors of Jules Chéret, the father of the modern poster. Bonnard's *France-Champagne* and Toulouse-Lautrec's *Moulin Rouge—La Goulue* were milestones in the history of poster art.

It is quite untrue to say that these artists were episodic and casual in their approach to poster art, even if Lautrec was not much concerned about the publicity content of his posters and used already existing designs. He chose the most suitable design for the purpose from his album; because of the originality of their composition and the placing of their well-defined chiaroscuro planes, many of his lithographs made ideal posters to which only the lettering needed to be added. Bonnard was more specifically committed, for he consciously intended to participate in the movement towards the applied arts then apparent in France and England; this was given theoretical expression by Morris and the 'Arts and Crafts' movement, and by the Secessionists in Vienna and Munich. A letter from Bonnard to Claude Marx, for example, demonstrates this point and gives an insight into the prevailing climate of radical transformation.

'Art for art's sake' already appeared anachronistic at a time when the royal houses of Europe were distributing prizes for the best industrial products at Exhibitions. When the demolition of the Eiffel Tower after the end of the Paris Exhibition of 1889 was proposed, there was a furore among artists.

In every European country there was renewed interest in the applied arts. As a result, a new relationship was formed between artists and society, and from the last years of the 19th century until the outbreak of the First World War, the so-called Decadent movement in art was accompanied by a belief in the revitalising of art, by an intense expectancy.

Meanwhile, due to the expansion of industry and the rise of a great consumer public, poster art had become a powerful propaganda medium; it had invaded the streets, participating in, influencing, and being influenced by, everyday life. It was employed to advertise new books, cabarets and circuses, and featured symbols and allegories of industrial progress in a variety of Art Nouveau styles; in form and content it reflected social changes. While Jules Chéret, the undoubted representative of Parisian industrial-middle class taste, continued to design his gay and always rather anecdotal posters, artists made their first attempts to transform the medium radically. Advertising became a part of everyday life, and a frenzied search for ways of beguiling clients and exploiting the acquisitive instinct had begun. While captive balloons with gigantic painted advertisements soared into the blue skies around Paris, poster companies tried to better the impact of the immobile wall-poster by employing sandwichmen and publicity carriages.

THE RISE OF POSTER ART

Jules Chéret

After credit has been given to the few but outstanding pioneering poster designs of Daumier, Bonnard, Vuillard and perhaps Degas (in his book *L'Affiche,* Lo Duca mentions a poster designed by him), one must inevitably consider Chéret's vast poster output;

10. Eugène Grasset. *Salon des Cent:* 1894. Bibliothèque des Arts Décoratifs, Paris.

10.   Eugène Grasset. *Salon des Cent*. 1894. Bibliothèque des Arts Décoratifs, Paris. The heavy outlining is suggestive of stained glass; the 'poetic' expression on the woman's face and the use of a plant motif are typical of Art Nouveau.

11.   Adolphe Willete. *Prenez du Cacao Van Houten*. 1896. Bibliothèque des Arts Décoratifs, Paris. © by SPADEM; Paris, 1967. Here Willette has abandoned his usual elegance of line and produced a soberly drawn robust Dutchwoman offering the product advertised and wearing her national costume.

12.   Edward Penfield. *Harper's Magazine:* February, 1894. Civica Raccolta stampe Bertarelli, Milan. The simplicity of the drawing makes the scene comprehensible at first sight: the essential quality of a good poster. Although the drawing is that of a book jacket, the lively colouring is that of a poster.

13.   Edward Penfield. *Harper's Magazine:* March, 1894. Civica Raccolta stampe Bertarelli, Milan. The March wind has made the young woman drop the magazine while attempting to keep her hat on; the white hare seems to be wondering how best to turn the situation to its own advantage.

11.   Adolphe Willette. *Prenez du Cacao van Houten.* 1896. Bibliothèque des Arts Décoratifs, Paris.

prenez du Cacao
Van Houten

12. Edward Penfield. *Harper's Magazine:* February, 1894.
Civica Raccolta stampe Bertarelli, Milan.

13. Edward Penfield. *Harper's Magazine:* March, 1894.
Civica Raccolta stampe Bertarelli, Milan.

what his admirer Maindron grandiloquently calls his *'oeuvre murale'*. In the course of his career, Chéret designed some thousand posters. In subject-matter they were enormously varied, including grand and comic opera, the ballets of the Folies-Bergère and dances of the Moulin Rouge, concerts at the Palais de Glace, book advertisements, the Musée Grevin, the great Parisian department stores, political journals, railways, seaside resorts, and various industrial and pharmaceutical products. To take only one example: between 1891 and 1904 Chéret made six different designs to advertise Saxoléine paraffin: a half-length figure of a dark haired woman seen in profile and turning to her left, wearing a green dress with a yellow rose in her bodice, regulating the light of a green-shaded lamp with her right hand . . . a half-length figure of a blonde woman . . . a full-length woman . . . etc., etc.

It is worth describing briefly Chéret's development as a poster designer, since it coincided with the development of lithography and chromolithography (discovered in 1836, the year of Chéret's birth), and since the quantity and technical perfection of his work have led to his being justly considered the father of the modern poster.

Maindron, who published many of Chéret's posters

in reproduction, has given useful information about his career. He learned the lithographer's trade from his father between 1855 and 1857, before designing his first posters. These have disappeared, and their titles are not recorded; it is only known that they consisted of some fifteen small designs (35×32.5 cm.) and were executed with pen on stone. After a stay in London (from 1859 to 1866) during which he perfected his typographic and chromolithographic techniques, Chéret returned to Paris. In London he had designed many covers for novels published by Cramer, and some twenty posters for operas, equestrian circuses and music-halls.

In Paris he opened a lithographic workshop; his posters were signed '*Imprimerie Chéret, n. 1 rue Brunel, Paris*'. In 1881, at the height of his powers, he handed over his printing press to M. M. Chaix & Cie but remained in control for obvious technical reasons, his posters now being signed '*Imprimerie Chaix (Succursale Chéret)*'. In 1890 Chaix merged the *Succursale Chéret* with his workshops in the Rue Bergère; the new signature was: *Imprimerie Chaix (Atelier Chéret)*. It is worth insisting at length on the relationship between artist and lithographic printer, which was integral to the technical and artistic development of the lithograph; this relationship ensured complete harmony between the colours and the artist's original drawing.

Chéret was the exponent of a transitional phase, which he interpreted with grace and, at times, a hint of the Art Nouveau manner then in vogue. The central motif of all his work was a full-bosomed eternal Eve with a dazzling smile full of *joie de vivre*. Perhaps he over-used it; but what else does most modern advertising, for all its computer research, opinion polls and hidden persuaders, amount to? Some of Chéret's posters are masterpieces of composition, for example the poster of 1896 for the Palais de Glace: its composition is cruciform, in the shape of a St Andrew's cross formed by two skaters passing each other; the woman in the foreground with her coat streaming open as though to suggest wings, sustained with cavalier elegance by the man behind her. Another Chéret poster (plate 2) features the word *Théâtrophone* in intense and almost phosphorescent red lettering with black shading, slightly curved against a deep blue background. The composition is in three planes. In the foreground a woman in yellow is listening through earphones; she is obviously interested and amused. Her arms, in long black gloves, are reminiscent of the long and expressive gloved arms of Yvette Guilbert —which makes a convenient transition to a consideration of Toulouse-Lautrec's powerful poster designs.

The Turn of the Century

It was to find a substitute for a Chéret poster that Zidler, the manager of the Moulin Rouge, asked his regular client, Toulouse-Lautrec, to design a poster for him. The result was the famous *Moulin Rouge— La Goulue* of 1891. As Edouard Julien, the keeper of the Museum of Albi, has remarked, this work at once demonstrated Lautrec's mastery of poster art; his ability to adapt the technique to his expressive intentions is astonishing. His posters are characterised by exciting colour contrasts, unusual arrangements of forms, audacious distortions and caricatures, unexpected dominant images, and a synthetic and energetic line softened by thick crayon outlines.

At the same time Willette, Ibels, Grasset, Mucha, Caran d'Ache, Forain, Cazalz and Sem were producing excellent poster designs in France; all the artistic tendencies of the age, from Symbolism to Art Nouveau, appeared in their work. It is difficult to consider late 19th-century poster art in other countries in isolation from that of France, which gave it birth; for the situation was much the same throughout Europe and the United States.

In Vienna and Munich the Secession movement and the Jugendstil, the German versions of Art Nou-

14. Ethel Reed. *Miss Träumerei.* 1895. Civica Raccolta stampe Bertarelli, Milan.

15. A. R. Gifford. *Womens Edition (Buffalo) Courier.*
Private collection.

14. Ethel Reed. *Miss Träumerei.* 1895. Civica. Raccolta stampe Bertarelli, Milan. A publisher's poster which combines the essential qualities of good taste and aggressive publicity content; note the great yellow chrysanthemums stretching diagonally across the composition.

15. A. R. Gifford. *Womens Edition (Buffalo) Courier.* Private collection. In this publisher's poster, French influence has given way before that of the Italian floral style. The gold background creates a compact colour plane that sets off the figure to good advantage.

16. Dudley Hardy. The *Chieftain.* Civica Raccolta stampe Bertarelli, Milan. The costumed figure and the title of the show have been associated in a single image with exceptional skill, and it is not surprising that this poster was published in *Les affiches étrangères* in 1897.

17. Dudley Hardy. *Abbotts Phit-Eesi Boots and Shoes.* Civica Raccolta stampe Bertarelli, Milan. The style of this poster artist is very English, as are the stances and gestures of the figures. The beautiful Art Nouveau lettering has been skilfully enclosed within the overall design.

THE CHIEFTAIN

BY
F.C.BURNAND
&
ARTHUR
SULLIVAN

SAVOY THEATRE.

16. Dudley Hardy. *The Chieftan* Civica Raccolta stampe
Bertarelli, Milan.

17. Dudley Hardy. *Abbotts Phit-Eesi Boots and Shoes*.
Civica Raccolta stampe Bertarelli, Milan.

veau, were paramount influences. Pioneers of poster art included Kolo Moser, E. Edel, Otto Fischer, Doepler and Kubik Franz Stuck; also Sattler, who created a fine poster for the Pan firm; Heine, who won a poster competition for the review *Simplicissimus;* and Zumbusch, who designed the poster for the review *Jugend.* Other outstanding poster artists were the famous *Jugend* group, six Munich poster designers —E. P. Glass, F. Heubner, C. Moss, E. Preetorius, M. Schwarzer and W. Zietara—and such others as Ludwig Hohlwein, a painter and architect who eventually became one of the most famous of the Munich poster artists. At work in Munich were Julius Klinger, the Expressionist Kirchner, and the painter, architect and interior decorator Henri van de Velde, a Belgian living in Germany; he was an outstanding theoretician, producing important ideas about the relationship between art and industry at a time when the machine was beginning to replace the craftsman, and also designed a splendid and widely influential poster (plate 24) for Tropon milk.

Poster art flourished in Belgium, as was demonstrated at the International Exhibition of 1894 and by the group around the *Libre esthétique,* for which Van Rysselberghe designed a fine poster. Other good posters were executed by Mignot (an artist in the style of Chéret, although more openly decorative), Donnay, A. Rassenfosse, Crespin and E. Berchmans.

In England, where the way had been prepared by Morris and the 'Arts and Crafts' movement, the classicism of design still evident in Fred Walker's poster (1870) for the Olympic Theatre soon gave way to Art Nouveau arabesques and derivatives of the Pre-Raphaelite style. Walker's black-and-white poster, which had been engraved on wood, was a precursor of the poster for Collins' *Woman in White,* and was apparently as successful as Lautrec's silhouette poster of Aristide Bruant. Aubrey Beardsley, the brothers Beggarstaff and others designed excellent posters, but the most successful artist of the period was the shrewd and humorous Dudley Hardy (plates 16 and 17).

In the United States fine posters were created by Edward Penfield, Ethel Reed, Will H. Bradley and A. R. Gifford.

Between the wars

Between the two World Wars, artists found new ways of expressing themselves: photo-montage, Cubism, geometric abstraction, *Fauvism* and other types of Expressionism, and so on. (Obvious examples are the

19. Alphonse Mucha. *Imprimerie Cassan Fils.* 1897.
Galleria del Levante, Milan.

20. Sem. *La Revue du Casino de Paris.* Bibliothèque des.
Arts Décoratifs, Paris.

18.   Alexandre Steinlen. *Cabaret du chat noir.* 1896. Civica Raccolta stampe Bertarelli, Milan. The cat in this poster inspired Anatole France to write in 1903: 'This tranquil and magnificent cat which threw the haughty shadow of its broom-like tail over Paris for many years, this cat which seemed so used to the gutters of Montmartre and certainly did not have the air of having escaped from some witches' sabbath, was the cat of Alexandre Steinlen. . .'

19.   Alphonse Mucha. *Imprimerie Cassan Fils.* 1897. Galleria del Levante, Milan. The floral style and Art Nouveau have here been combined in an allegorical design in which the central scene is surrounded by lettering and scrolls.

20.   Sem. *La Revue du Casino de Paris.* Bibliothèque des Arts Décoratifs, Paris. © by SPADEM; Paris, 1967. Sem was so successful in giving the illusion of movement in this poster that one almost expects to see the Scots dancers disappear behind the curtain and reappear from the other side of the stage.

21.   Manuel Orazi. *La Maison Moderne.* Bibliothèque des Arts Décoratifs, Paris. © by ADAGP; Paris, 1967. In this poster the Art Nouveau style has achieved a rare degree of coherence. The design and placing of the lettering, counterpointing the woman's silhouette, emphasises the stillness of the composition.

21. Manuel Orazi. *La Maison Moderne.* Bibliothèque des Arts Décoratifs, Paris.

analytic posters of Cassandre and Cappïello's 'arab-esque'.) Such variety was not easily absorbed; and it was in reaction against the over-allusiveness and intellectualism of many posters that the German Lucian Bernard made his poster-objects.

Notable examples of German poster design included a poster by Willi Künze for the Railway Centenary of 1937, a poster by Zepf for the Zeppelin, Zietara's humorous poster for the Munich Carnival, and posters by the Expressionist, Engelmann. Many outstanding poster artists were active in Belgium, including Michel Olyff and Jacques Riches, who designed an excellent poster for Gevaert Films.

The American-born Edward McKnight Kauffer was the outstanding poster artist working in Britain between the wars. He was fully aware of modern trends in art, having studied in Chicago and Paris, and abandoned his career as a painter only in 1921, when he had already been established as a poster artist for some years. He himself said, 'In 1919 I produced the first and only Cubist poster design in England', *The Early Bird* for *The Daily Herald*.

For the most part, however, Kauffer's work was more eclectic, exhibiting the influence of, among others, the French painter Fernand Léger. Kauffer's most famous poster is probably *London History at the London Museum,* first published in 1922, in which the flames of the Great Fire of London are rendered in a style very like that of Vorticist paintings, with areas of flat colour and clean, hard lines. The poster was republished in 1966 (the three-hundredth anniversary of the fire), and was again a great success.

Although some adventurous designs were also made by Aubrey Hammond, F. C. Herrick, George Massiot and others, most British posters continued to be executed in a detailed, naturalistic style; typical of superior work of this kind were the posters by Sir Frank Brangwyn and other recognised painters of the old school. For this state of affairs the caution of clients was more to blame than artistic conservatism, as was demonstrated by the work produced under the aegis of a few enlightened patrons like London Transport and Shell.

The greatest popular and commercial successes of the period were humorous or whimsical: H. Harris's *Bovril prevents that sinking feeling,* with its bemused man in pyjamas astride a bottle of Bovril in the middle of the ocean; Will Owen's *Bisto Kids,* two ragamuffins in caps, ravished by the odour of Bisto gravy; and John Gilroy's *My Goodness, My Guinness* series, in which the precious Guinness stout is put at risk by the balancing tricks of a friendly seal. Other British poster artists who produced work of distinction included Purvis, Cooper, Newbould, Wadsworth, Taylor, Bawden and Ashley.

Adolphe Mouron, who signed his posters A. M. Cassandre, worked mainly in Paris and occasionally in New York. His success was such that he was called 'the street's first stage-designer'. Whereas the Italian Cappiello, who worked with equal success in Italy and Paris, might be called a Fauve, Cassandre was very definitely a Cubist. (Obviously such terms can only be used in this context to indicate a general tendency.) From his first posters, for the *Casquette Grand Sport* (1926), Cassandre made use of elements of Cubist painting, elegantly emphasising the object to be publicised, in this case the sporting cap: the face of the man with the pipe in his mouth is suggested by a geometrical white outline.

In 1927 Cassandre produced one of his most successful posters, in which the plasticity of the design was combined with a really exceptional poetic element: the *Etoile du Nord*. The shining platform extending into the far distance, the pale and unsettling blues, and the star in the background are wonderfully suggestive of the romance of travel.

In 1932 Cassandre won one of his greatest successes with *Dubo . . . Dubon . . . Dubonnet* (plate 53), in which

22. Adolf Hohenstein. *Tosca.* 1899. Civica Raccolta stampe Bertarelli, Milan.

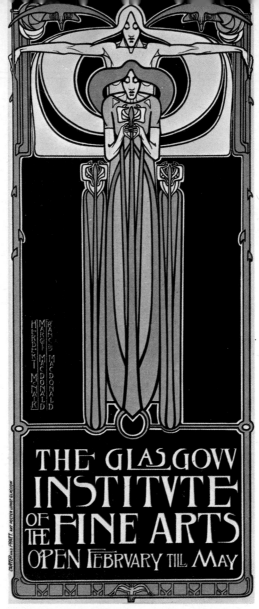

23. H. McNair, M. and F. Macdonald. *The Glasgow Institute of the Fine Arts*. 1896. Private collection.

24. Henri Van de Velde. *Tropon.* Museum für Kunst und
Gewerbe, Hamburg.

22.   Adolf Hohenstein. *Tosca.* 1899. Civica Raccolta stampe Bertarelli, Milan. This gigantic poster has been justly considered Hohenstein's masterpiece because of its plastic qualities and symbolic colouring. The spirit of melodrama has been communicated by means of appropriately theatrical techniques: notice Tosca's huge shadow and the serpent entwined around one of the letters of her name.

23.   Herbert McNair, Margaret and Frances Macdonald. *The Glasgow Institute of the Fine Arts.* 1896. Private collection. A design in which the linearism of Art Nouveau is taken to its limit and touched by a hint of mystical Gothicism.

24.   Henri Van de Velde. *Tropon.* Museum für Kunst und Gewerbe, Hamburg. A splendid piece of Art Nouveau. The dominant plant motif suggests the waves of the sea. The lettering is particularly successful here, whereas on several other Art Nouveau posters it was almost illegible.

25.   Leopoldo M. Metlicoviz. *Inauguration of the Simplon Tunnel. International Exhibition.* 1906. Ricordi Collection, Milan. Printed by the Officine Grafiche Ricordi. This poster combines two contrasting elements to produce a single effect: the allegorical figures perched on the front of the locomotive and the impressive moment of exit from the Simplon tunnel into the blinding light of the sun.

25. Leopoldo M. Metlicoviz. *Inauguration of the Simplon Tunnel. International Exhibition.* 1906. Ricordi Collection. Milan.

the drinker is shown in three different stages of enjoyment, against coloured backgrounds suggestive of his mood. In 1935 Cassandre created yet another masterpiece: the character 'Nectar' for Nicolas wines (plate 52). The bottles are placed in the centre of a labyrinth of lines in movement which in some respects anticipate Op Art techniques. Cassandre became well-known on both sides of the Atlantic, and he received important commissions from *Fortune* and *Harper's Bazaar;* in Italy he was commissioned by Dino Villani for designs for the poster *Il dolce che sa di primavera,* and for the Motta dove which has appeared on Italian walls and hoardings in the last few years.

In France, contemporaries and successors of Cassandre included Jean Carlu, Paul Colin, Charles Leupot, Léon Gischia, Jean Lurçat, Jacques Nathan, J. P. Junot, Hervé Morvan, Bernard Villemot and André François. Jean Carlu is considered one of the masters (and theoreticians) of the French poster; his output has been prolific. Some of his important works are the poster of 1934 for the Aquarium of Monaco (plate 51), the poster for the Cousine Electrique (which became a neon-lit silhouette after dark), and the highly successful mosaic of flags broken by a white profile for the Paris International Exhibition of 1937.

Paul Colin designed splendid posters, including

one of 1938 (for the Musée de l'Homme, Paris) with the profile of an Easter Island statue in burnt ochre painted against a white background. Léon Gischia, a painter and stage designer, made use of photomontage and colour in highly personal style.

In 1933 Cassandre met the young Savignac, who became his collaborator for several years. Raimond-Pierre Guillaume Savignac was born in Paris in 1907; the string of Christian names which he liked to reel off are an indication of his particular brand of humour. Like many other excellent poster designers, he began as a draughtsman. In 1933 he became Cassandre's collaborator, but his own posters found no takers despite the support he received from an intelligent publicity agent. It was only in 1949, after a small exhibition held jointly with his colleague Bernard Villemot, that he sold his first poster, *Mon Savon;* this was the prelude to his great successes. In 1952 a very successful Savignac exhibition was organised at the Galleria d' Arte Moderna. The introduction to the catalogue says: 'Milan has the pleasure of presenting, in the quiet rooms of the Gallery of Modern Art, the clamour of Savignac's posters. He has avoided facile success and has never been content merely to accept the prevailing fashion. He sold his first poster at the age of forty . . .

'Behind each of his posters are precise ideas and a power of synthesis which enhances instead of killing the vitality of the image. A Savignac poster has the simplicity of a page from a child's primer: few words and highly simplified ideographic drawing . . . As in primers, the colour is chosen to ensure the complete 'legibility' of the publicity idea; it is the work of a refined artist who has thoroughly understood modern painting.' And since a tradition of caricature exists in France alongside, and related to, the intellectual tradition (one need only recall the mordant style of Siné or the ironic tenderness of Paynet) it is not difficult to understand Savignac's success. His humour is wide-ranging and capable of encompassing intellectual ideas and simple fun; the clarity and cohesion with which they are treated explains his enduring success.

Italian Posters

The slow development of poster art in Italy was perhaps in part the result of the struggle for unity and independence, and of Italy's industrial backwardness. The same struggle had, however, brought about the production of notices, proclamations, political caricatures, and portraits of heroes of the Italian Risorgi-

26. Ernst Ludwig Kirchner. *Brücke 1909*. Straatliche
Graphische Sammlung, Munich.

26. Ernst Ludwig Kirchner. *Brücke 1909.* Staatliche Graphische Sammlung, Munich. Kirchner, who was a painter, sculptor and graphic artist of the Expressionist school, composed his posters with strong flat tints and thick wood-cut lines.

27. Ludwig Hohlwein. *Richard Strauss-Woche.* Museo teatrale della Scala, Milan. Because of their high quality and rigorously controlled style, Hohlwein's posters often transcend their original function as advertisements, as in this example, which deserves inclusion in any anthology of poster art.

28. Leonetto Cappiello. *Le Thermogène.* 1909. Bibliothèque Nationale, Paris. © by SPADEM; Paris, 1967. With Thermogène, Cappiello succeeded in creating an advertising character, the 'fire-spitting *pierrot',* who became the symbol and trademark of the product for sale.

29. Leonetto Cappiello. *Cinzano.* 1910. Ricordi Collection, Milan. © by SPADEM; Paris, 1967. The idea of presenting the product dynamically and unusually has been perfectly executed in this example: the half-naked rider mounted on a striped horse and brandishing a bottle instead of a sword in a scene which is somehow not in the least absurd.

30. Leonetto Cappiello. *Bitter Campari.* 1921. Civica Raccolta stampe Bertarelli, Milan. © by SPADEM; Paris, 1967. The red imp, the same colour as the Campari, is wrapped in a spiral of orange peel; he is one of those advertisement characters who become identified with the product advertised.

27. Ludwig Hohlwein. *Richard Stauss-Woche*. Museo teatrale della Scala, Milan.

28. Leonetto Cappiello. *Le Thermogène*. 1909. Bibliothèque Nationale, Paris.

29. Leonetto Cappiello. *Cinzano*. 1910. Ricordi Collection, Milan.

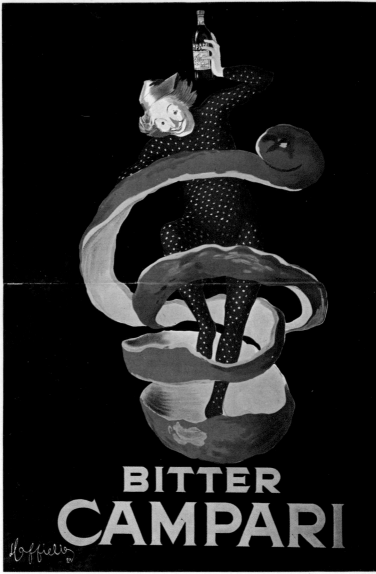

30. Leonetto Cappiello. *Bitter Campari*. 1921. Civica Raccolta stampe Bertarelli, Milan.

mento (these in particular tended to be printed in lithography and chromolithography).

The great age of the Italian poster begins with bills advertising grand opera; these acquired special characteristics which clearly set them apart from posters for variety shows, music halls or circuses. Contemporary with them were the first posters commissioned by industry. G. M. Mataloni, a designer who had started as a lithographer, brought out a fine decorative poster for the Auer incandescent lamp in 1891—one of the first posters printed by the firm of Ricordi.

This was the beginning of a successful and prosperous period for Ricordi; for twenty-five years they produced almost all the great posters of this, the great age of the Italian poster. The firm displayed its shrewdness in setting up a workshop and inviting a group of artists to work for them. The director was Adolf Hohenstein, the oldest of the group, which worked side by side with the printers, just as Chéret had done.

The series of posters made by Ricordi for the Mele department stores of Naples deserves separate mention; between 1896 and 1915 hundreds were designed and printed. They appeared with each new season and were written about by Eduardo Scarfoglio. The poster artists were Cappiello, Dudovich, Metlicoviz, Terzi and Sacchetti. A picture of these days has been given by one of the leading poster artists, Marcello Dudovich. At the age of seventy-five he wrote a brief memoir called *Nostalgia* (1953). 'At the age of fifteen I came from Trieste to Naples and had the good luck to be taken on straight away as an apprentice in the workshop of Metlicoviz, who was the head of a printing department of the Ricordi firm. In those days Giulio Ricordi, that unforgettable Maecenas . . . had gathered round him the best poster artists of the time, paying them generously for their work for the famous firm where posters were printed with designs by Villa, Cappiello, Mataloni, Metlicoviz and Hohenstein.'

The Ricordi firm published posters by Dudovich, Mauzan, Nomellini, Terzi, Sacchetti, Palanti and Franz Laskoff, the last-named an émigré from St Petersburg. Laskoff's liking for animals is evident in two of his most memorable posters: a clumsy but likeable polar bear who lies on his back, quenching his thirst with Cordial Campari (poster of 1906); and two quarrelling pups struggling for possession of the Borsalino cap (1908). The same firm printed one of Hohenstein's masterpieces in 1899: a giant poster (plate 22) for Puccini's *Tosca* with a melodramatic play of light and shade and a serpent coiled around one of the Art Nouveau letters. In the same year he designed

31. Leopoldo M. Metlicoviz. *Cabiria*. 1912. Ricordi
Collection, Milan.

32. Marcello Dudovich. *Marca Zenit*. 1910. Ricordi Collection, Milan.

33. Marcello Dudovich. *Mele & C. Mode e Novità*. 1912.
Ricordi Collection, Milan.

31. Leopoldo M. Metlicoviz. *Cabiria*. 1912. Ricordi Collection, Milan. Printed by the Officine Grafiche Ricordi. Metlicoviz was inspired by D'Annunzio's emphatic and rhetorical style in this dramatic poster with red flames about to engulf the strange, boyish body of the woman.

32. Marcello Dudovich. *Marca Zenit*. 1910. Ricordi Collection, Milan. Printed by the Officine Grafiche Ricordi. This elegant and natural advertisement for gloves, walking stick and black bowler hat won Dudovich the *Zenit* competition of 1910.

33. Marcello Dudovich. *Mele & C. Mode e Novità*. 1912. Ricordi Collection, Milan. Printed by the Officine Grafiche Ricordi. Dudovich introduced a simple but effective publicity idea: admiration of the model by the couple on the right. The model, dressed in pink, stares straight at the spectator.

34. Achille Lucian Mauzan. *Fate tutti il vostro dovere!* 1917. Civica Raccolta stampe Bertarelli, Milan. The soldier's pointing finger seems almost three-dimensional, partly because of his hypnotic stare: from whatever angle the spectator looks at the poster, he is fixed by these eyes. The poster was immensely popular.

a poster for Monowatt which featured a female nude and a cluster of lamps. As we may see, the two great themes of Italian poster art, opera and industry, were already present in perfect harmony. In 1899 Leopold Metlicoviz designed a poster for Mascagni's opera *Iris,* with a female face surrounded by irises in Art Nouveau style; in 1912 a flaming red poster for the Italo-Film production *Cabiria;* in 1914 the unforgettable figure of a red woman set asymmetrically against a hazy grey background—a poster for the Calzaturificio di Varese.

In his memoirs Dudovich wrote, 'It was while living in such an atmosphere that my passion for posters was born, and after a hard apprenticeship which culminated with the winning of the Borsalino Prize, I moved to Bologna from Chappuis. From there I went to Munich, after being invited to become a permanent collaborator on *Simplicissimus.* I would still be there but for the outbreak of the First World War.' The competition mentioned by Dudovich was perhaps the first Italian publicity competition for posters and products, offering big prizes: 2500 lire for the first prize, 1000 lire for the second. Another winner was the Sicilian poster artist Aleardo Terzi. Terzi's development was meteoric, and after some posters with highly refined colouring and allegorical figures he made two designs which are very important in the history of Italian poster art: the monkey brushing its teeth with Dentol (plate 36) and the puppy with a paint brush in its mouth for the Colorificio Italiano Max Meyer & C. (plate 37). The 238 posters and 643 products invited to take part in the competition were exhibited at the Society for Fine Arts under the title *Prima Esposizione di manifesti-réclame e di disegni per marchi di fabbrica nazionali* ('First exhibition of advertising-posters and designs for national products'). It was visited by twenty thousand people and, according to the press, was the first applied arts exhibition to assume greater importance than an exhibition of fine art.

Poster art, in Italy as elsewhere, attracted painters and sculptors because of its technical novelty and the scale on which the artist could work. Among them were Luigi Conconi; Leonardo Bistolfi, who designed the poster for the Turin exhibition of modern decorative arts in 1902; Romolo Romani, who died prematurely leaving two splendid unpublished sketches (70 × 100 cm.) for Bitter Campari now in the Civic Gallery of Modern Art in Brescia; Aroldo Bonzagni, who brought his own provocative brand of caricature into poster design; Bignami, Palanti, Nomellini, Caldanzano and Aleardo Villa. The poster designers proper, led by the eldest, Hohenstein, included Mataloni, Metlicoviz, Terzi and Sacchetti. Sacchetti was a strong draughtsman who designed excellent posters with highly refined but effective contrapuntal colour tones. Examples are his poster for Bitter Campari (1921), with the figure of the bon-viveur in green against an orange background; and his poster of 1904 for the Unione Cooperativa, with an elegantly dressed lady standing in an autumn wind which blows dead leaves about her.

The initial, authentic style of these poster artists was that of Art Nouveau, with profuse employment of symbols; but artists were already beginning to develop a more modern synthetic style. Other designers continued to work in an academic vein, or in the rhetorical style known as *dannunziano*. This was the style of such artists as De Karolis, creator of a magnificent giant poster (140 × 200 cm.) for *La Figlia di Jorio,* inspired by a well-known painting. Guido Marussig, the stage designer for D'Annunzio's *Nave* and the designer of the heraldic emblems and other decorations in the Vittoriale, was also capable of working in a robust, plastic style.

Another important designer working in Italy was the Frenchman Mauzan, a talented but uneven artist

35. Enrico Sacchetti. *Bitter Campari*. 1921. Ricordi
Collection, Milan.

35.   Enrico Sacchetti. *Bitter Campari*. 1921. Ricordi Collection, Milan. Printed by the Officine Grafiche Ricordi. Setting the livid, elegant bon-viveur against an orange background creates a vibrant colour contrast. The poster very successfully conveys the feeling of well-being given by drinking the aperitif.

36.   Aleardo Terzi. *Dentol*. 1914. Ricordi Collection, Milan. Printed by the Officine Grafiche Ricordi. After the languid colour contrasts of his early Art Nouveau posters, Terzi used a more synthetic design and colouring. The idea of the advertisement is no longer suggested but direct: the monkey hanging from a tree and brushing its teeth with Dentol is so amusing that, once seen, it is never forgotten.

37.   Aleardo Terzi. *Colorificio Italiano*. 1921. Ricordi Collection, Milan. Printed by the Officine Grafiche Ricordi. The scene of the puppy with a paint-brush in its mouth and a remorseful air at having upset the tin of paint was so effective that it became the trademark for Max Meyer's firm, Colorificio Italiano.

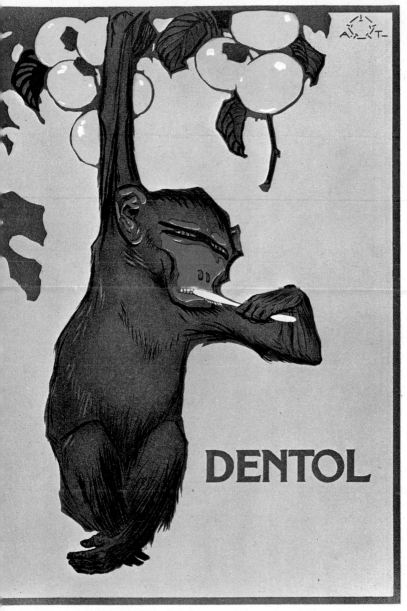

36. Aleardo Terzi. *Dentol.* 1914. Ricordi Collection, Milan

37. Aleardo Terzi. *Colorificio Italiano*. 1921. Ricordi Collection, Milan.

whose output was enormous. His best work has great expressive power. It is sometimes almost repellent: three undernourished figures with huge noses greedily sniffing a piece of Parmigiano Bertozzi cheese; the contrast between a tiger's fangs and the teeth of a young woman in the advertisement for Avoriolina Bertelli; and the series of large posters for Italian silent films. But Mauzan's most famous work was the poster (plate 34) for the National Loan, featuring a soldier in the trenches who points directly at the spectator to illustrate the caption: Everyone must do his duty! (The poster of course had English parents and French relatives.) According to Guido Rubetti, one version of this poster measured thirty metres square; the head of the soldier alone was three metres wide. Each poster weighed over six pounds. They were put up on the facades of all the great public buildings of Italy.

Others who made important contributions to Italian poster art were Sinopico, Nanni and Depero. In his subtle linear designs on a black background, the Futurist Depero apparently broke the elementary rules of poster art; he nonetheless created some excellent posters, for example a famous poster for Bitter Campari and an excellent one for the Unica Easter Egg. Nanni worked with topical themes; one of his recent posters for Campari shows a bottle transformed into a Sputnik in orbit around the earth. Also worth mentioning are Mazza, who designed a symbolic poster for the re-opening of the Bocconi department stores under the name of Rinascente; and Codognato, especially for his poster celebrating the crossing over the Simplon Pass by aeroplane.

At the beginning of the twentieth century, poster design had begun to take on its modern aspect, simple bold motifs replacing the 'picture' or 'illustration'. Artists increasingly sought to identify the product advertised with a thematic figure or object. One of the protagonists of this tendency was Leonetto Cappiello, who remarked that he knew one of his posters was a success when customers asked for 'Red Horse Chocolate' instead of Chocolat Klaus. Cappiello was born at Leghorn in 1875 of Neapolitan parents, and was a Parisian by adoption although he continued to work in Italy. In 1901 he created a poster to advertise Leghorn as a seaside resort: a woman dressed in jade-green, and the lettering spelled out on illuminated children's balloons. In 1903 he published the Chocolat Klaus poster, which made a sensation because of what we would now call the flat, rubber-stamped colours: the red horse, the woman in jade green, with yellow hair against a black background. In 1909 another strikingly novel and influential design appeared, featuring the character Thermogène pierrot, who became the incarnation of the product (plate 28). Less than a year later Cappiello designed his splendid poster of a striped horse carrying a rider with a bottle (plate 29). In 1921 came the two Robba pierrots drinking out of the same cup. This poster was distinguished by the extreme refinement of its drawing and use of greys; the two pierrots form almost a heraldic emblem. In 1932 he brought out a marvellously audacious black-and-white poster for *La Merveilleuse*.

Ironically enough, just as the Frenchman Mauzan won his greatest triumph in Italy (the National Loan poster), so Cappiello was always most successful in France. In 1929, for example, he designed a poster for Ocap shampoo that anticipated Savignac's style, and in 1930 one for Bouillon Kub (plate 46); both were masterpieces, establishing striking visual and analogical relationships between subject and lettering.

An Italian who was making his reputation in France at the same time was Severo Pozzati, who returned to Italy to found a poster school at Leghorn. He signed his posters 'Sepo', and one of his first successes was in Paris with a poster (plate 43) for the man's collar Noveltex, which won a prize in New York. It was clearly influenced by the Bauhaus and the geometric compositions of Cassandre. As Churchill has related, Sepo clandestinely designed another version of this poster in 1944—with *Present!* in large letters, to salute the Allies' entry into liberated Paris.

In 1929 he designed a poster for Sardines Amieux, a confidently stylised design with light green, blue, turquoise and violet colouring; a white sardine is shown swimming, the slogan *toujours à mieux* in red lettering on its back. Picasso asked to meet Sepo and asked him for a copy of the poster. It became so popular that it even inspired a satirical song.

Sepo's success in Paris was henceforth assured. A French critic wrote: 'For the second time a poster designer of the first order has come from Italy to put his talent at the service of publicity. The first . . . was Cappiello. The second, as you will have guessed, is Sepo.'

In Italy, where he was commissioned by Dino Villani (who had already commissioned Cassandre's Easter dove poster) Sepo designed his poster for Motta Panettone. Since then, the fragrant and inviting pieces of *panettone* set against the red background of the initial M have appeared on Italian walls every Christmas.

Only a few years after entering the publicity depart-

1) Если белогвардейщину недобьем совсем
2) Белогвардейщина снова встанет на ноги.
3) Если пана добьем и сложим руки
4) Руку к рабочему протянет Врангель.
5) Пока не укрепится красное знамя, — винтовка не может быть нами брошена.

наркомпрос роста №149.

38. V. Mayakovsky. *Mural Newspaper No. 49.* 1920.
Private collection.

НА КОНЯ РАБОЧИЙ И СЕЛЯНИН!
КРАСНАЯ КАВАЛЕРИЯ—
    ЗАЛОГ ПОБЕДЫ!

39. Anonymous. *To horse, workers and peasants! The Red cavalry is the guarantee of victory!* 1919. Lenin Museum, Moscow.

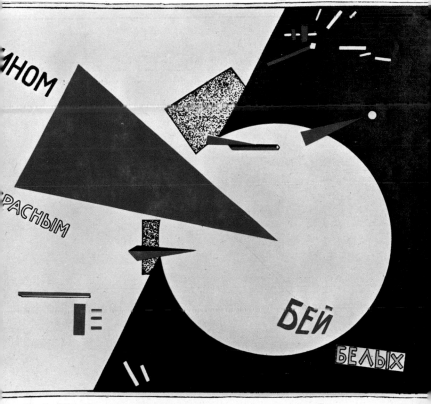

40. L. Lisitsky. *With the red wedge hit the whites!* 1920.
Private Collection.

38.   V. Mayakovsky. *Mural newspaper no. 49.* 1920. Private collection. The poster was part of the series *Satirical windows of the Fanlight:* 1) if we don't finish with the White Guards 2) the White Guards will rise again; 3) if we don't finish with the *pan* 4) Wrangel will strike out at the working man; 5) until we have consolidated the red flag 6) we won't be able to throw away our guns.

39.   Anonymous. *To horse, workers and peasants! The Red cavalry is the guarantee of victory!* 1919. Lenin Museum, Moscow. Published at Kiev. Its elegant and lively design glorifies the combative spirit of Budyenny's famous cavalry corps.

40.   L. Lisitsky. *With the red wedge hit the whites!* 1920. Private collection. Lisitsky, a graphic artist and architect, was one of the leaders of the Russian Constructivist movement. His poster demonstrates his faith in the symbolic power of expression of geometrical shapes.

41.   S. Ivanov. *First of May. Long live the festival of the workers of all lands!* 1920. Lenin Museum, Moscow. The allegory of Spring strewing flowers over the workers' procession conveys something of the social and cultural enthusiasm of the early years of the Russian Revolution.

42.   A. Kadakov. *The illiterate is like a blind man: failures and accidents await him at every step.* 1920. Lenin Museum, Moscow. The poster is drawn and composed as though it were a popular print, and illustrates the caption simply and effectively.

41. S. Ivanov. First of May. *Long live the festival of the workers of all lands!* 1920. Lenin Museum, Moscow.

 КНИГИ

42. A. Kadakov. *The illiterate is like a blind man: failures and accidents await him at every step.* 1920 Lenin Museum, Moscow.

ment of the firm of Perugina Buitoni, Federico Seneca leaped into the front rank of poster designers. His 1928 posters, of the green nun (plate 45) and the child's head against a green background for Pastina Glutinata Buitoni, are famous. In the introduction to the album of Seneca's posters published in 1952, Borgese has given a description of this artist's posters with which I entirely agree: 'His great posters appeared unexpectedly, with authority, power and weight; they were intense, classical and pure; surprising and persuasive because they were classical; simple and monumental because they were harmonious and balanced . . . Seneca became the foremost actor in the theatre of the street . . .'

After World War II, though he showed signs of flagging, Seneca continued to play a part in poster design with his posters for the ENI; his triptych *Pibigas illumina, Pibigas riscalda, Pibigas cuoce* ('Pibigas lights, Pibigas heats, Pibigas cooks'); and, also for Pibigas, a poster with a striped cat watching its flaming tail, which appeared in every Italian street.

In poster art, as in painting, there were a number of 'naïve' artists who achieved dazzling results. One such was Ercole Giommi, who designed a poster (plate 44) with a highly effective slogan using a popular saying: *Apri l'occhio! Per la salute Acqua Giommi!*

('Open your eyes! Acqua Giommi for health!'). A few years earlier, in 1924, Marcello Mizzoli designed a poster for the firm of OM which featured a darting red automobile which seemed to be shooting straight out of the poster towards the spectator. He also designed posters for the Milan Fair, for Fiat Lubricants, and for the exhibition of decorative arts at Monza (1930). In 1931 he produced his two masterpieces for Bitter Campari and Cordial Campari, utilising some Cubist techniques and borrowing elements of Sironi's style. His interest then turned to industrial design and architecture. He worked for Olivetti, and produced some excellent posters for the firm.

In the years between the wars, a technical transformation began which was also to influence the aesthetics of poster design. Lithography and chromolithography were replaced by photo-mechanical reproductive processes in which the exact colour prescribed by the artist was almost always obtained, by means of superimposed filtered colours. After the Second World War there was a new flowering of the poster art. Space forbids treatment of the post-war work of Dudovich and a whole series of young and not-so-young designers, including Ricas, Munari, Cavadini, Ciuti, Mosca, Carboni, Testa, Dinelli, Giovanni Pintori (who gave Olivetti's publicity such distinction—see plate 63—creating several posters which must be regarded as indispensable anthology-pieces), Gian Rossetti, Cremonesi, Bonino, Franco Grignani, Castiglioni, Tovaglia and Benca.

POSTER TECHNIQUES
AND INFLUENCE

The basic form of the poster, as has been remarked, developed in the second half of the 19th century. It was no coincidence that this occurred during the Third Republic in France and the great urban trans-formation of Paris which had been begun by Baron Haussmann. This connection between poster art, urbanism and architecture—and later decoration and the applied arts—was a constant one.

Even if we admit that the posters of Toulouse-Lautrec are in a category of their own, it is difficult to agree with C. M. Santini that they were not particularly significant in the development of poster design. After all, Lautrec's poster-work consists of more than sim-plification for the purposes of the medium. His use of strong, flat tones, and his ability to add lettering to the composition (harmoniously, yet without reducing its legibility), prove that he was a consummate poster designer. His attention to this point can be seen in the three versions of *Aristide Bruant dans son cabaret*. (Chéret, by contrast, inserted his lettering directly or superimposed it on the picture later.

After Toulouse-Lautrec, it was no longer possible to design quasi-naturalistic 'painterly' posters like Chéret's; Lautrec's flat colour planes, his refusal to model figures with chromolithographic dots, and his use of tone obtained by sprinkling, were important lessons for poster artists. His contribution to the development of poster design was decisive.

The relationship between poster art and 'culture' became more conscious, and the new awareness led to the participation of poster artists in the Art Nouveau movement (and, later, in other *avant-garde* movements). Art Nouveau not only had an enormous influence on architecture, the applied arts and interior decoration, but also affected the graphic arts—and especially poster design.

Cappiello was more inclined towards the world of the Gay Nineties—mingling the occasional hint of Symbolism with a discreet suggestion of Art Nouveau —than towards the Secessionist style; but before the Art Nouveau period had ended he was designing posters with large colour planes. 1903 was a decisive date in his development, for it was then that he designed the poster for Chocolat Klaus with a great

43. Sepo (Severo Pozzati). *Noveltex*. 1928. The artist's collection, Bologna.

43. Sepo (Severo Pozzati). *Noveltex*. 1928. The artist's collection, Bologna. The motif is given maximum emphasis in this poster by means of the geometric composition and the black and red colour contrast. A clandestine version of the poster, to which the word *Present!* was added, was posted up on the walls of Paris on the day the Allied troops entered the city in 1944.

44. Ercole Giommi. *Apri l'occhio!* 1928. Giommi Collection, Milan. The poster is effective because the name of the product advertised is associated with a popular saying (Open your eyes!'). The expressive and elementary graphic composition of the poster has affinities with that of the *naïf* school of painting.

45. Federico Seneca. *Pastina Glutinata Buitoni.* 1929. The artist's collection, Milan. An example of an apparently improvised idea-synthesis by Seneca in his 1920s period. The effect is very striking.

44. Ercole Giommi. *Apri l'occhio!* 1928. Giommi
Collection, Milan.

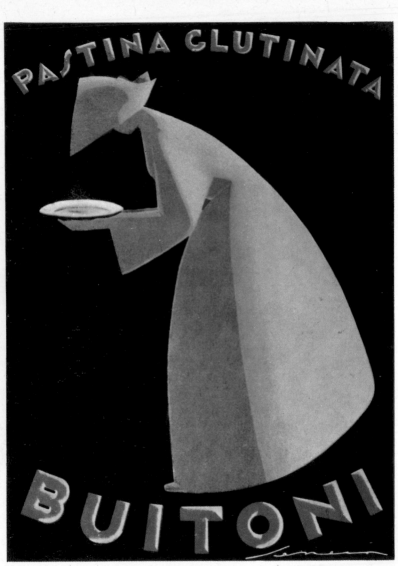

45. Federico Seneca. *Pastina Glutinata Buitoni.* 1929.
The artist's collection, Milan.

central nucleus of colour. This was influential in lettering as well as in drawing in the years before World War I. Cappiello had abandoned the sensual curvilinearism of Art Nouveau for an imagery and simplicity that anticipated the *lettrism* of the Futurists and Cubists.

In the early post-war years, the *avant-garde* movements began to develop again. In Munich, the Belgian architect and painter Van de Velde, who had settled in Germany, arrived at a definition of the proper relationship between art and industry which was to be the basis of Gropius' Bauhaus programme. The Bauhaus produced Herbert Bayer's scientifically Surrealist posters and Moholy-Nagy's rationally composed abstract posters. These influenced European graphic art and then, after the advent of Hitler and the closing down of the Bauhaus had led to the emigration of Gropius, Bayer and Moholy-Nagy, art in the United States.

Berlin in the early 1920s was the birthplace of photomontage, which was to have tremendous influence on graphic art and poster design. This was invented by the Dadaist John Heartfield as a means of expression more objective than the traditional medium of painting. The name 'photo-montage' was bestowed on the invention by Grosz, Haussmann, Hoech, Baader and

Heartfield (the author of the manifesto *The Hand Has Five Fingers,* now considered a classic). Although there must inevitably be omissions and approximations in such comparisons, it is not difficult to detect the influences of Constructivism and Dadaist photomontage in the magnified propaganda posters of the early Russian Revolution, and in posters for the Soviet cinema.

With regard to figurative art (and even intellectual fashions), French poster art showed itself highly receptive to influences, not only because French poster design was based upon a solid tradition, but also because the work of the best designers—Cassandre, Colin, Carlu, Gischia, Villemot, Savignac—reveals acute intellectual curiosity. Hence the French poster is the richest in echoes and reflections—and sometimes banalisations—of modern artistic styles and techniques: *collage;* Cubist geometry and fragmentation and interpenetration of forms; the simplified contours of Léger; the unusual colours of Matisse; the fantasy of Chagall, the geometry of Mondrian, the feverish brush-strokes of Dufy . . .

After World War II the use of other media for advertising—television, radio, cinema—challenged the poster. But the dialogue in the streets (a dialogue without hindrance or obligation) between retailer and

46. Leonetto Cappiello. *Bouillon Kub.* 1930. Bibliothèque des Arts Décoratifs, Paris.

46. Leonetto Cappiello. *Bouillon Kub.* 1930 Bibliothèque des Arts Décoratifs, Paris. © by SPADEM; Paris, 1967. The theories of the 'arabesque' which had been so dear to Cappiello gave way to more clear-cut and pricise ideas of visual and analogical communication. Although a similar 'synthetic' style was anticipated on a German poster by Ottler, this is undoubtedly a masterpiece.

47. Marcello Dudovich. *Pirelli.* 1930. Civica Raccolta stampe Bertarelli, Milan. Dudovich overcame the difficulty of combining two disparate elements in the design by setting the woman inside the tyre. The impression of high speed is given by the way the woman's scarf streams out, covering her eyes.

48. Marcello Nizzoli. *Campari.* 1931. Civica Raccolta stampe Bertarelli, Milan. Nizzoli was inspired by 20th-century painting, especially the weight and incisiveness of Sironi's painted objects. There is also a discreet hint of Cubist interpenetration of planes.

49. Mario Sironi. *L'Ambrosiano.* 1934. Ricordi Collection, Milan. The distortion of the newspaper-seller's figure, contrasted with the tiny street-lamps, is characteristic of the particular blend of expressionism and sentimentality comprising Sironi's style.

47. Marcello Dudovich. *Pirelli*. 1930. Civica Raccolta stampe Bertarelli, Milan.

48. Marcello Nizzoli. *Campari*. 1931. Civica Raccolta stampe Bertarelli, Milan.

49. Mario Sironi. *L'Ambrosiano*. 1934. Ricordi Collection Milan.

consumer proved to be irreplaceable: poster artists struck out in new directions, paying greater attention to the techniques of industrial design, artistic experiments (for example action painting) and the many other visual experiments. Today the direction of exchange between poster art and 'fine' art seems to have been reversed in certain respects, and many typically graphic characteristics have made their way into painting, especially Pop Art.

Two seconds to take in a poster

'The idea is the salt of the poster . . . The idea is the egg of Columbus . . . Columbus's discovery was how to suppress the egg-cup. The poster is an optic scandal. You don't want to look at it yet you see it. Its form is determined by the laws of optics. It must be read instantaneously. A good poster hides the wall on which it is stuck as a good actor makes you forget the stage on which he stands. The poster is the jest that replaces a lengthy discourse. The poster is essentially something ephemeral . . .'

Natanson said of the first appearance of Toulouse-Lautrec's posters, that the miracle would not be repeated, and remarked that a poster was not made to yellow in libraries but to be stuck on a wall, to become torn and rain-splashed.

Savignac, whose posters remove banality from the commonplace, was in a sense trying to make us understand the qualities essential to a good poster; Natanson was indirectly stressing the value of the factor of surprise in a poster. Both agree that a poster must be seen out-of-doors.

Dino Villani defined the poster poetically, as a 'paper siren'; Cassandre described it more prosaically as a 'publicity telegram'. But it is evident that all kinds of psychological, technical and aesthetic factors are involved in an attempt to define the poster's function; for instantaneous communication by means of an abstract sign or image is the basis of the alphabet. Today it is not only the chief aim of poster designers and publicity technicians, but also of many *avant-garde* artists, to study communication techniques.

Advertising experts claim that a poster that cannot be absorbed in two seconds flat is not a good poster. But of course the time factor will vary with human feelings and situations: waiting, boredom, haste, desire, enthusiasm, surprise, etc., give a dimension different to that of chronometric time. It is precisely these variants that the good poster designer must

50. Paul Colin. *Bravo. L'hébdomadaire du spectateur.* The artist's collection, Paris.

51. Jean Carlu. *Aquarium de Monaco.* 1933. The artist's collection, Paris.

50.   Paul Colin. *Bravo. L'hébdomadaire du spectateur.* The artist's collection, Paris. © by ADAGP; Paris, 1967. Of Colin's posters it has been rightly said that 'they give a strong impression through the senses and a clear idea through the spirit.' In this poster for a weekly theatrical magazine, the idea of the auditorium has been identified with the public's cry of *Bravo!* and has been communicated with robust simplicity.

51.   Jean Carlu. *Aquarium de Monaco.* 1933. The artist's collection, Paris. The evocation of underwater life is splendid; the whole composition, down to the little bubbles around the lettering, is suggestive of the aquatic.

52.   Cassandre. *Nicolas.* 1935. The artist's collection, Paris. © by ADAGP; Paris, 1967. 'Nectar', the legendary Nicolas character, seems to be be emerging from a wine cellar painted by a modern Op artist. The eye-catching play of lines and colours makes this an extremely effective poster.

53.   Cassandre. *Dubo. . . Dubon. . . Dubonnet.* 1932. The artist's collection, Paris. © by ADAGP; Paris, 1967. It has been said of this poster that 'only the blind are ignorant of Dubonnet'. The obsessive rhythm of the three parts of the poster makes it an unforgettable design.

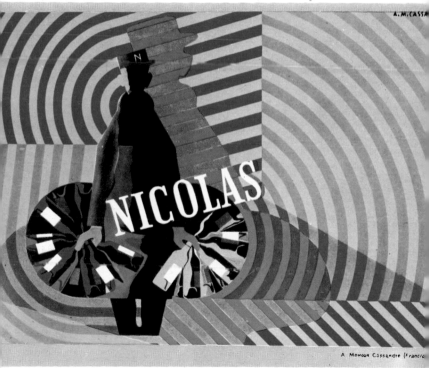

52. Cassandre. *Nicolas.* 1935. The artist's collection, Paris

intuitively perceive and know how to use. (It is significant that Mallarmé studied the effectiveness of the distribution of blacks and whites in posters and newspapers, and the comparative intensity of typographical characters.)

One of the greatest difficulties of poster design lies in gauging the speed with which an idea is recognised when it has been translated into a more or less institutionalised sign or more or less legible metaphor. Eventually a sign may become so institutionalised that it replaces language altogether—for example the arrow, the simplest of all directional signs. Another example is the outline of a hand with index finger outstretched. (Steinberg exploited the instant recog-

nition accorded this conventional directional sign in his uncaptioned drawing of a pointing finger with a bandage round it to indicate a hospital.) When the symbol or image is too well-known, the element of surprise is lost; when it is insufficiently familiar, it is not immediately comprehensible.

Scientifically speaking, all sorts of other factors are involved: the physiology of the eye, the psychological impact of colour and shape, etc. In reality the artist does not attempt to solve his problems along these lines—which is just as well, since the scientific approach raises as many questions as it provides answers. The talented poster artist always finds his own best way of expressing himself. Cappiello dis-

53. Cassandre. *Dubo . . . Dubon . . . Dubonnet.* 1932. The artist's collection, Paris.

54. John Gilroy. *Guinness celebrating the coronation of Elizabeth II*. 1953.

55. Tom Eckersley. *After work, Guinness.* 1961.

ESPAÑA

GOYA

Ligereza y temeridad
de Juanito Apiñani
en la plaza de Madrid
grabado de LA TAUROMAQUIA
1815

56. Goya. *Dexterity and temerity of Juanito Apiñani*. 1965.
Rossi Collection, Milan.

57. K. Reys. *Plaza Toros, Cordoba*. 1951 Rossi Collection,
Milan.

PLAZA TOROS CÓRDOBA

DOMINGO **21 DE OCTUBRE DE 1951**, a las TRES de la tarde, se celebrará

UNA MAGNA CORRIDA DE TOROS HISPANO-MEJICANA

organizada por la Comisión Municipal PRO-MONUMENTO A MANOLETE

Se picarán, banderillearán y serán muertos a estoque

10 ESCOGIDOS TOROS, 10

CEDIDOS GENEROSAMENTE POR LOS AFAMADOS GANADEROS

Excmo. Sr. DUQUE DE PINOHERMOSO · D. Félix BARTHOLOME · Sres. Herederos de GALACHE · D. Arturo Sánchez COBALEDA · D. Alipio Pérez T. SANCHON
D. Leopold L. de CLAIRAC · Excmo. Sr. CONDE DE LA CORTE · D. Hermelano DIQONICHEZ · D. Juan BELMONTE · D. Carlos ARRUZA y D. José de la COVA

El PRIMERO de ellos
REJONEADO por el **Excmo. Sr. DUQUE DE PINOHERMOSO**

LOS NUEVE RESTANTES ESTOQUEADOS POR

ARRUZA · PARRITA · CAPETILLO · MARTORELL · SILVETI
CALERITO · APARICIO · LICEAGA y LAGARTIJO

Tanto el rejoneador como los espadas y sus cuadrillas, actúan en esta corrida desinteresadamente
Los toros de los tres ocho estarán dedicados a las ocho de las picos de Córdoba   La Plaza estará adornada con gallardetes y banderas nacionales de España y Méjico

SOMBRA, 100 PESETAS · SOL, 50 PESETAS

PARA MAS DETALLES VEAN PROGRAMAS DE MANO

La ofrecen su Jerez semilla: o MORILES o MONTILLA   Ganado de origen: CONDE DE REGALADO   IMP. y LIT. ORTEGA - VALENCIA

54.   John Gilroy. *Guinness celebrating the coronation of Elizabeth II.* © Arthur Guinness Son & Co., 1953. The Guinness animals were so well-known and loved that it was not even necessary to identify the advertiser.

55.   Tom Eckersley. *After work, Guinness.* © Arthur Guinness Son & Co., 1961. A key figure in British poster design, Eckersley continues the excellent Guinness tradition, but replaces Gilroy's representational style with carefully chosen ideographs.

56.   Goya. *Dexterity and temerity of Juanito Apiñani.* 1965. Rossi Collection, Milan. With the symbolic addition of red, Goya's etching from the *Tauromachia* series has been used as part of a poster of great distinction.

57.   K. Reys. *Plaza Toros, Cordoba.* 1951. Rossi Collection, Milan. A typical bull-fight poster in two parts: the classic scene of the matador making passes with his red cape, and the lettering section with different type used for the various *corridas.*

58.   Savignac. *Il Giorno.* 1956. Civica Raccolta stampe Bertarelli, Milan. In this design Savignac has been completely successful in realising his aim of immediate and total impact.

59.   Armando Testa. *Carpano.* 1950. The artist's collection, Turin. One of a successful series of 'historical' posters. Notice the clever use of collage, with various decorative elements from the label of the vermouth appearing on the king's cape.

58. Savignac. *Il Giorno*. 1956. Civica Raccolta stampe Bertarelli, Milan.

59. Armando Testa. *Carpano*. 1950. The artist's collection, Turin.

covered what he called his 'arabesque-idea', Savignac relied on his unfailing humour, and so on. Of all the more or less contradictory statements about psychic and physical sight, one thing is certain: the subject that least loses its 'legibility' is the human figure: man instinctively recognises himself in even the most highly stylised or idealised representations. Another vexed question has been where posters should be displayed; this remains undecided, and is perhaps not very important.

Travel Posters

The travel poster has a complex of cultural, social and sporting functions in addition to its immediate commercial and industrial functions. Such a multiplicity of functions is inevitable since a travel poster cannot publicise the sea, the snow or museums without advertising the comfort of hotels, and cannot extol the speed and comfort of various means of transport without glamorising destinations. The first travel posters appear to have been made to advertise spas. For the present purpose, however, origins are of less interest than the general development of this type of poster and the question of what its tasks are today.

Tourist agencies, sea and air companies, railways

and so on provide opportunities for the use of the 'leisure time' of the masses—something which did not exist before the 19th century, deriving from increased earnings, reduced working hours and technical progress. The development of the bicycle, for example, produced such posters as Toulouse-Lautrec's famous advertisement for a bicycle chain, and a curious allegorical design (1903) by Emilio Malerba for the Bicicletta Stucchi (it featured a naked woman with one foot on a pedal). Next came allegories of speed, with pictures of the first motor cars and the first aeroplanes, with pilots shown throwing flowers. But the dominant motifs of travel posters are inspired by man's age-old inexhaustible wish to travel and discover.

After a dull start and a few resounding failures, travel poster design has become highly developed— with particularly interesting results in Switzerland, Italy and France and, more recently, Japan. In Switzerland, excellent designs have been made by Herbert Matter, Walter Herdeg, Herbert Leupin and Donald Brun. Herdeg's poster for *St Moritz* is unforgettable: the great snowdrop makes a kind of tapestry pattern around the only lettering in the design—the name of the place—and in the photo-montage the watchman guides the sun over the snow-field to help the skier.

60. Herbert Leupin. *Coca-cola*. The artist's collection, Basle.

60.   Herbert Leupin. *Coca-Cola*. The artist's collection. Basle. The absent musician, gone to wet his throat after playing the trumpet, and the notice with its play on words (pause—trink—think—drink), make this a very entertaining and effective piece of work.

61.   Donald Brun. *Gauloises*. The artist's collection, Basle. The extreme simplicity of the design, the use of areas of flat colour, and the stylisation of the cock (which suggests the nationality of the product) produce a very pleasing effect.

62.   Marcello Nizzoli. *Olivetti Lexicon*. 1950. Civica Raccolta stampe Bertarelli, Milan. The bird, evidently singing the name 'Lexicon', is as elegant in design as the machine itself. Excellent advertising.

63.   Giovanni Pintori. *Olivetti Elettrosumma 22*. 1956. Olivetti, Milan. The graphic translation of the working of an *Elettrosumma* has here become a kind of game which hides the product.

64.   Gui/do (Guido Stefanini). *L'inglese per chi viaggia e chi lavora*. 1965. Civica Raccolta stampe Bertarelli, Milan. This poster, which was deservedly given a prize, may be read in two seconds since the precise ideographic image is a suggestive metaphor of Englishness.

61. Donald Brun. *Gauloises*. The artist's collection, Basle.

Lexikon

olivetti

62. Marcello Nizzoli. *Olivetti Lexicon.* 1950. Civica Raccolta
stampe Bertarelli, Milan.

Olivetti Elettrosumma 22

63. Giovanni Pintori. *Olivetti Elettrosumma 22*. 1956. Olivetti, Milan.

l'inglese

PER CHI VIAGGIA E CHI LAVORA

in edicola il numero 1 col 1° disco

FRATELLI FABBRI EDITORI

64. Gui/do (Guido Stefanini) *L'inglese per chi viaggia e chi lavora.* 1965. Civioa Raccolta stampe Bertarelli, Milan

ART TODAY The Tate, re-hung with taste and logic, offers the academically approved, the Whitechapel the young and middle-generation painters. The Greater London Council sets contemporary British sculpture against the simpler pleasures of Battersea Park. Complete your survey with the commercial galleries of deepest Mayfair and Chelsea, and the avant-garde extremes. For all these new frontiers, the explorer's kit is simple—an open mind, Underground and bus maps, and a sense of humour. For The Tate Gallery: Underground or bus to Westminster, then bus 77B. For The Whitechapel Art Gallery: Underground to Aldgate East. For Battersea Park: Underground to Sloane Square, then by bus 137.

65. Hans Unger. *Art Today.* 1966.

In France, Cassandre designed his splendid *Etoile du Nord* in 1927 and *Wagon Lit* in 1930. He created many posters for seaside resorts and sea voyages, including a monumental composition of 1935 featuring the liner *Normandie,* its great bulk suggesting security as it glides over a calm sea; the peace of the scene is broken only by a flight of seagulls.

Many good travel posters have been designed in Italy: Dudovich made an eloquent design to advertise Lake Como, setting the silver outline of the lake against a world map. Xanti Schavinsky composed a joyous photographic poster entitled *Summer on the Sea* (1934) for a cruise organised by the Italia-Flotte Riunite. Carlo Dradi made a series of successful posters for the Ferrovie Nord; the most striking, a poster inviting fishermen to come to the Ticino region, shows the rear of a train transformed into a fish's tail. Nizzoli's poster for the city of Milan was a striking *collage* of the spires of the Cathedral.

Many of the best British travel posters since the First World War have been produced for London Transport, which has been (and, for that matter, continues to be) an outstanding and enlightened patron. One executive, Frank Pick, commissioned posters from McKnight Kauffer as early as 1915-1916; and, largely through Pick's initiatives, not

e grafica safgra

s.p.a./milano

66. Erberto Carboni. *Arte Grafica Safgra*. 1953. Safgra Collection, Milan.

65.   Hans Unger. *Art Today* © London Transport, 1966. London Transport have commissioned designs from important painters and sculptors as well as the best poster artists. Hans Unger's design is a witty mock underground 'map' of modern art.

66.   Erberto Carboni. *Arte Grafica Safgra.* 1953. Safgra Collection, Milan. An abstract to advertise a printing firm: the message is implicit in the skilful design and the high quality of the printing.

67.   Attilio Rossi. *Son et Lumière.* 1959. Civica Raccolta stampe Bertarelli, Milan. A poster in which the different rays of coloured light, as in a *son et lumière* show, highlight a famous historical monument.

68.   Henryk Tomaszewsky. *Henry Moore Exhibition.* 1959. International Biennale of Poster Art, Warsaw. This poster for an art exhibition is of an extreme refinement. The general appearance of Moore's sculptures, particularly his predilection for 'holes', is graphically suggested by the letters of the artist's name.

69.   Jan Lenica. *Alban Berg Wozzeck.* 1964. International Biennale of Poster Art, Warsaw. The form of this poster is reminiscent of Art Nouveau. Lenica has constructed a face by means of lines and colours which suggest the dodecaphonic music of Berg and the terrible story of the opera.

67. Attilio Rossi. *Son et Lumière*. Civica Raccolta stampe Bertarelli, Milan.

68. Henryk Tomaszewsky. *Henry Moore Exhibition.* 1959
International Biennale of Poster Art, Warsaw.

69. Jan Lenica. *Alban Berg Wozzeck*. 1964. International Biennale of Poster Art, Warsaw.

only the best British poster artists but also most of the important painters and sculptors—Sutherland, Nash, Piper, Roberts, Epstein—designed posters for London Transport.

Theatre Posters

Posters advertising amusements or plays have a place of their own in the history of the commercial poster. Chéret designed posters for every kind of amusement, but especially for the theatre of varieties; Toulouse-Lautrec designed his few but important posters for the Moulin Rouge. Other early examples of the art include huge and picturesque circus posters which seem imbued with a spirit of hyperbole not unlike that of modern Pop Art paintings.

Italy, the home of opera, was the birthplace of a new type of poster which replaced the typographic opera poster with white paper, scrolls and friezes. As G. Veronesi said, 'this type of poster has its own history—a history that is wholly Italian.' These opera posters have the qualities and defects of the figurative art of the time; in Italy this was mostly of the anecdotal, more or less realistic or Impressionist type. The motifs were derived from the libretti, and were often climactic episodes of the plot, the colouring assuming chromatic qualities inspired by the music. One example is Hohenstein's masterpiece (plate 22) for the *première* of Puccini's *Tosca* (1899) at the Teatro Costanzi at Rome. Tosca is bending over the dead Scarpia amid a play of dramatic light and shade contrasts, and intense red, olive, yellow and black tones. In 1913 Plinio Nomellini produced a poster for Mascagni's *Parisina,* an opera with a libretto by D'Annunzio. Parisina stands among deep velvety shadows in the depths of a prison cell lit by the flicker of flames outside. In 1910-1911, Giuseppe Palanti designed a poster for Puccini's *Girl of the Golden West* and in 1912 a splendid poster for Mascagni's *Isabeau:* a young woman on a white horse, her flowing hair and the horse's mane bathed in a golden light among a profusion of mists and roses. Inevitably, Verdi's first centenary inspired many poster designers, including Codognato, Ballerio, and Metlicoviz, who designed two excellent posters. One, announcing the inauguration of a monument to Verdi and performances of *Traviata* and *Falstaff* conducted by Toscanini, showed Verdi in full figure, silhouetted against a gilt ochre sky with a low horizon and a distant view of Busseto. The second was a less naturalistic design: Gemito's bust of Verdi, painted in white against a dark green background framed by laurel wreaths.

Two posters that would delight even the most

hardened collector were discovered recently. One was for Gounod's *Faust*, and represents Marguerite at her spinning wheel between the young Faust and Mephistopheles. In format the poster is in a transitional stage between the typographic and the illustrated poster. It was, however, printed in lithography by the firm of Rossetti and dated 'Milan 1862'—that is to say, before Chéret went to London to perfect his lithographic techniques. The other (1874) was a curious graphic *capriccio* for the opera *Salvator Rosa,* with a group of small multi-coloured figures; Vesuvius is in the background. The scene is surrounded by the florid lettering of the period.

Prose drama has occasioned a number of fine posters, like that for the Piccolo Teatro di Milano by Muratore, who also made posters for Brecht's *Threepenny Opera* and *Galileo Galilei* and Chekhov's *Platonov*. The cinema, on the other hand, has only rarely inspired good poster design. An exception was Stahl-Arpke's masterpiece for *The Cabinet of Dr Caligari*.

Posters for art exhibitions

The book *102 Posters* records the important exhibition 'Twenty-Five Years of Posters for Art Exhibitions',

Z MAKEDONIE, SRBSKA, CHORVATSKA,
SLOVINSKA, BOSNY A HERCEGOVINY
A ČERNÉ HORY
V PROVEDENÍ MAKEDONSKÉHO
PĚVECKO - TANEČNÍHO SOUBORU ZE SKOPJE
UMĚLECKÝ VEDOUCÍ DUŠKO GEORGIEVSKI

70. Jaroslav Sura. *Pisné a Tance Jugoslavie*. 1966. The artist's collection, Prague.

70. Jaroslav Sura. *Pisné a Tance Jugoslavie.* 1966. The artist's collection, Prague. In this Czech poster for a performance of Jugoslav songs and dances, the ideographic stress is upon the song. Notice the successful use of lettering on the bird's body to suggest feathers.

71. Hiroshi Tanaka. *Recruitment of blood donors.* 1966. International Biennale of Poster Art, Warsaw. This won the first prize for the social section of poster art in the Warsaw Biennale of 1966. The graphic ideogram and its symbolic colouring make the message unmistakeable.

72. Ben Shahn. *He says NO to civilization and survival.* The artist's collection, Rooswelt, New Jersey. An election poster. The American painter Ben Shahn has represented Goldwater as a baby holding one foot in his hand. The repetition of the spectacles obviously represents a mannerism of Goldwater's. The singularity of the composition makes up for the absence of the direct impact of the classic poster.

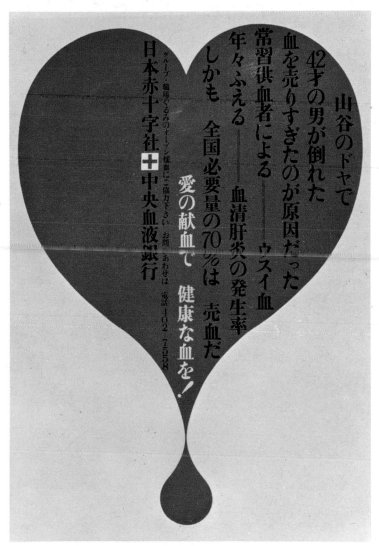

71. Hiroshi Tanaka. *Recruitment of blood donors.* 1966.
International Biennale of Poster Art, Warsaw.

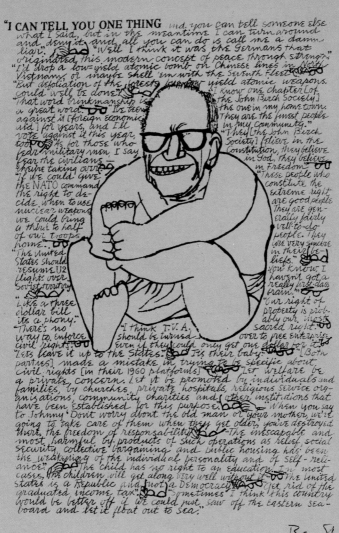

72. Ben Shahn. *He says NO to civilization and survival.*
The artist's collection, Rooswelt, New Jersey.

which took place at the Galerie Kléber in 1952. The poster for this exhibition was designed by Matisse (plate 73), and the original work (an abstract *collage* with splendid contrapuntal use of colour) was hung beside the printed poster.

This kind of poster was, of course, more than twenty-five years old. Gavarni, Grandville and others designed posters to announce exhibitions of their book illustrations and etchings; in 1890 Chéret designed a poster to advertise an exhibition of his pastels, drawings and poster sketches; and an exhibition in Paris of *Affiches Artistiques,* held in the Salon des Centenaires in 1890, was announced by a poster by Toulouse-Lautrec. But, these exceptions aside, the poster designed by the artist-exhibitor himself dates from the sensation aroused by Jacques Jaujard's printing of some posters for the Louvre which included colour details of several masterpieces.

The posters produced by this stimulus were original lithographs in their own right, since the artists themselves drew on the stone or, more rarely, on transfer paper, and patiently supervised the printing. Some, like Picasso, haunted the workshop for months on end, and in 1954 Braque went right across Paris to see a single colour proof. Mourlot said of Léger that he was 'a born poster designer. He had all the gifts of synthesis, force and vivacity.' His works had certain constant characteristics: a central illustrated theme and variations in the kind of lettering; typographical characters are sometimes used when the letters are not drawn by the artist himself. The latter were the most harmonious in effect, though it must be admitted that the typographical characters are always cleverly inserted in the composition.

In the volume mentioned, and in the Galerie Maeght, there is a variety of posters designed by Braque, Chagall, Matisse, Picasso, Léger, Miró and other artists. They are all lithographs proper, free from all photo-mechanical processes of reproduction and even the softness of chromolithography. The compositions are dominated by the artist's own hand-drawn lines and a free, joyous use of colour.

Picasso has designed many posters for his own exhibitions, and also for bull-fights organised by him in the south of France. He has made linocut posters for his exhibitions of ceramics and pottery at Vallauris, and also designed a poster for the exhibition '*Affiches Originales des Maîtres de la Pensée Française*'.

Gentilini and Marino Marini have recently designed posters for their exhibitions at Rome, held respectively in the Palazzo Barberini and the Palazzo Venezia (plates 75 and 76).

Political posters are so numerous as to require a separate book. The first popular posters, with their sowers of seeds of knowledge, torches of liberty and broken chains, were succeeded by some good satirical posters and the brief but glorious period of early Soviet poster art with its large photo-montages, the satire of the poet Mayakovsky (plate 38) and the Constructivism of Lisitsky (plate 40).

Closely related to these are war posters: the posters of the First World War; Käthe Kollwitz's proletarian manifestoes; Heartfield's photo-montages; the posters of the Spanish Civil War, which first showed a thunderstruck world the faces of children killed by bombing; Second World War posters; and so on. Perhaps none was as effective as those recently designed to protest against the atomic bomb, the finest being the Czech Vaclav Sevcik's poster with the single word No! and a great mushroom cloud of skulls, and the poster by Henrion, with a skull transformed into a mushroom cloud.

POSTER ART TODAY

Since the Second World War, posters have had to take their place among a whole battery of other publicity media, though they still keep their own special function. In some countries, for example Switzerland and Japan, schools of poster art have been established to explore all the possibilities of the medium, from abstract design to the most objective form of representation. The chief Swiss designers are Donald Brun, Leupin, Hans Herni, Hans Looser, Piatti, Butler and Manfred Maier.

In the United States, publicity has developed other means and techniques, but despite the relative scarcity of posters, excellent graphic designs have been made by Saul Bass, W. H. Allner, Paul Rand, Joseph Binder, Will Burtin, Leo Lionni and Herbert Bayer. Others, like Gyorgy Kepes and the painter Ben Shahn (creator of several magnificent posters, including the one reproduced in plate 72), have been experimenting with new visual techniques. Many experimental studies have been carried out in communication techniques and poster art.

Some of the most important innovations in poster design have been made in the Communist countries, where there is no commercial publicity. Far from drying up, poster art has been of very high quality in these countries, and especially in Poland, where there was already a splendid graphic tradition. Among the leading artists are Ladisla Sutnar, Willi Rotter, and Ota

matisse 52

AFFICHES D'EXPOSITIONS RÉALISÉES DEPUIS 25 ANS
PAR L'IMPRIMERIE MOURLOT ET PRÉSENTÉES A L'OCCASION
DE SON CENTENAIRE A LA GALERIE KLÉBER, PARIS
, AVENUE KLÉBER - 5 DÉCEMBRE 1952 - JANVIER 1953

73. Henri Matisse. *Affiches d'expositions à la Galerie Kléber.*
1952. Galerie Maeght, Paris.

73.   Henri Matisse. *Affiches d'expositions à la Galerie Kléber.* 1952. Galerie Maeght, Paris. © by SPADEM; Paris, 1967. For the centenary of his famous printing firm, Mourlot held an exhibition of posters designed by well-known artists. Matisse composed the lively collage for the poster reproduced here.

74.   Pablo Picasso. *200 Works from 1920 to 1953.* Rossi Collection, Milan. © by SPADEM; Paris, 1967. Two of Picasso's greatest paintings, his *War* and *Peace,* were exhibited on this occasion. Picasso designed this dramatic gesture of despair for the poster as an evocation of his two famous works.

75.   Franco Gentilini. *Exhibition at the Palazzo Barberini.* 1965. Galleria del Naviglio, Milan. With its almost graphic design, Gentilini's painting makes the basis for a by no means contemptible poster.

76.   Marino Marini. *Exhibition at the Palazzo Venezia.* 1966. Galleria Toninelli, Milan, Marini's horses are by far the most famous of his sculptures. Here, the tersely drawn horse and rider anticipate and complete the written message.

77.   Ivan Ripley. *Black Flower.* © Big-O Posters Ltd., 1968. The sale of posters to the general public has recently become a flourishing business. This decorative example of the new poster art is ostensibly advertising the idea of 'flower power'.

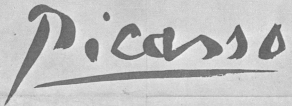

200 OPERE DAL 1920 AL 1953

GALLERIA NAZIONALE D'ARTE MODERNA

ROMA - VALLE GIULIA MAGGIO GIUGNO 1953

74. Pablo Picasso. *200 Works from 1920 to 1953.* Rossi Collection, Milan.

75. Franco Gentilini. *Exhibition at the Palazzo Barberini*. 1965. Galleria del Naviglio, Milan.

76. Marino Marini. *Exhibition at the Palazzo Venezia.*
1966. Galleria Toninelli, Milan.

Janacek (who in 1948 designed a beautiful poster, featuring the sun and a bull, for an exhibition of Spanish painters of the School of Paris). Polish poster art is now enjoying a golden age like that of the Soviet poster during and for a few years after the October Revolution.

With the aid of the government, Polish designers organised an International Poster Biennale held in Warsaw in 1965. A collection of the best posters of 1964-1965 was displayed, with nine prizes assigned to the best posters in three categories: social, cultural and advertising. The three first prizes went to the Japanese Hiroshi Tanaka for his social poster *(Recruitment of Blood Donors*, plate 71), to the Pole Jan Lenica for his cultural poster *(Wozzeck*, plate 69), and to the Japanese Kazumasa Nagai for his advertising poster for Hasahi beer.

Humour remained a prime ingredient of the British poster. Tom Eckersley devised the famous *Good Mornings begin with Gillette*, in which the hairy and the clean-shaven of various species confront each other with mild astonishment. Eckersley also worked for Guinness, for whom so many excellent posters have been designed; plate 55 replaces the representational style of Gilroy with carefully chosen ideographs.

Hans Unger has favoured a 'cartoon' style with thick lines and areas of flat colour with ragged edges, as in his posters advertising *The Observer's* American and Russian columns. *Art Today* (plate 65) is in a very different style, reminiscent of Léger, with a witty mock underground 'map' of modern art.

F. H. K. Henrion's designs are notable for their strong rhythms, and have appeared to particular effect in posters for airlines, petrols, etc. But one of Henrion's best is his *Philishave* poster, in which the nose, smiling mouth, round head and arms of a half-shaved man form a continuous spiral which admirably conveys the movement and speed with which the electric razor operates.

Such effects are achieved by neither chance nor unaided inspiration: one of the leading post-war British designers, Abram Games, has described the severe analytical effort required to combine or superimpose apparently unrelated images without sacrificing coherence of mood. That analysis is not destructive of humour is demonstrated by such designs as Games's *Keep Britain Tidy*, with a cheeky dustman sitting on his cart in 'Britannia' pose, broom held at arm's length.

Lack of space makes it impossible to do more

than name the creators of some of the best work in the last decade: Dennis Bailey, David Gentleman, Robin Walton, Reginald Mount, Colin Banks, Robert Claxton. Many more deserve to be mentioned.

In recent years all obstacles to experiment have been swept away. Non-naturalistic art has become acceptable to an ever-widening public—especially when, in posters, television commercials, cartoons and similar media, it is not presented as 'art'. As one fashion after another has been superimposed on —rather than superseding—its predecessors, commercial art has become increasingly eclectic: Pop, Op, Art Nouveau, the photograph, photo-montage, typographical and cartoon styles are employed at will, singly or in combination.

Whether motivated by public taste or their own compulsions, many modern artists strive to create works with the kind of instant claim on the attention that characterises poster art. It is therefore appropriate that the poster should have acquired a new role and a new status. This originated with the American and British 'underground' (hippies, flower people, etc), from which came a flood of posters, mostly in an extravagantly floral neo-Art Nouveau style (see plate 77). Some advertised events or propagated ideas, but many were clearly

77. Ivan Ripley. *Black Flower*. 1968.

intended to be displayed simply as works of art; they were 'posters' because they were mass-produced by the same process as the equivalent objects devoted to public persuasion.

The popularity of this idea ensured its rapid commercialisation, and the sale of posters directly to the public has become a flourishing business. What has always been regarded as the most transient of the 'applied' arts appears to be assuming a second role as a 'fine' art.

'A beautiful poster gives immortality for twenty-four hours', a German poster artist has remarked; but his statement is contradicted by the mounting number of collectors, publications and exhibitions.

LIST OF ILLUSTRATIONS   Page